The Dedalus Press

Torso of an Ex-Girlfriend

Gerry Murphy

TORSO OF AN EX-GIRLFRIEND

GERRY MURPHY

DEDALUS

The Dedalus Press
24 The Heath ~ Cypress Downs ~ Dublin 6W
Ireland

© Gerry Murphy and The Dedalus Press, 2002

Acknowledgements:
The author wishes to thank Karen McEnery, Mick McCarthy,
Gregory O'Donoghue, Patrick Galvin, Fiona Barry and Jack Healy.
Some of these poems have previously appeared in "The Shop",
"Southward", "Compost" (Boston), "Poetry Ireland Review" and
"De Brakke Hond" (Belgium)

ISBN 1 901233 90 1 (paper)
ISBN 1 901233 91 X (bound)

Dedalus Press books are represented and distributed in the U.S.A.
and Canada by **Dufour Editions Ltd.**, P.O. Box 7, Chester
Springs, Pennsylvania 19425
in the UK by **Central Books**, 99 Wallis Road, London E9 5LN

The Dedalus Press receives financial assistance from
An Chomhairle Ealaíon, The Arts Council, Ireland.

Printed in Dublin by The Johnswood Press

CONTENTS

AS FOR DANTE

Halfway along my appointed way,
whistling cheerfully in a vast forest,
I strayed hopelessly from the path.

What the forest was like,
how increasingly silent, how exquisitely dark,
even now I shudder to remember.

for Katherine O' Donnell

A Vote of Thanks

OK,
two years in the wilderness
then a new muse appears,
beautiful and impenetrable,
thanks

Plato.

SELF-PORTRAIT AT 46

There is my penis,
gathering fluff
beneath the soft horizon
of my underpants

BALLYNOE HAIKU

My kisses like bees
in your honey coloured hair
sweetly mistaken.

Your kisses like rain
on the forgotten desert
of my abdomen.

Sweet Burden of Memory

Almost forgotten
then I wake up to find you
sitting on my face.

HONEY

There's none can tell
how much I missed
your pouting, bee-stung lips,
which look as if
you kept your mouth
hard pressed against
a hive's busy entrance
all Summer long.

LONG SUMMER AFTERNOON
(for Gráinne)

(i)

As you sleep,
your tanned pelt
glowing against lemon sheets,
a warm southern wind
whips a sprinkling of rain
through the open window:
A blind cartographer
mapping you with kisses.

(ii)

In the name of memory,
I claim that quicksilver
trickle of sweat;
its sinuous track
down into the small
of your back;
its slight tickling
at the top
of your buttocks;
its happy drip
into fragrant darkness.

(iii)

Three days,
two showers later,
your smell fades
from my skin
and I submerge without trace
in the grubby quotidian.
Then, one morning,
several weeks after,
I pull on my grey sweater —
the very one you pressed
into service as a nightgown —
and suddenly inhale you
all over again.

POET AND MUSE
(after Goethe)

Once, while you slept,
I lay wide awake
in your arms,
working on an ode
in your honour,
fingering out the rhythm
along your back.

WATER MYTH
(for Patricia)

"Whatever inspires,"
you call from the shower,
the water stunned into droplets
on your suddenly delicious skin.
"Well," I reply,
from the airport
twenty seven years later:
"even with arms,
in your presence
the Venus de Milo
would be queueing
to be kissed."

THE O'NEILL SUITE

(i) WOOD SPRITE

In the afternoon quiet
of the café,
in the green-gold light
of your company,
a light flickering down
through dense canopies of leaves
to glimmer on the forest floor
of your deeply untroubled mind.

(ii) CAHERLAG

It was late
and I wanted to talk quietly
to your heart,
but the wind
was chasing its tail
through the trees along the avenue,
the rain was trying out
a new syncopation
on the bins in the yard
and a sudden tumult of voices
in my head drowned out
your disconcerting aria.

(iii) BEMUSED

This morning,
your voice on the radio;
your face at the bottom
of the cereal bowl
I have been trying to fill;
your smile in the glint
on the handle of the tea cup;
your neck in the fluted stem
of the juice-stained glass
I have been twisting and twisting.

(iv) BALANCING ACT

I have been trying
to forget you,
in eight other arms,
seven legs.
But it's useless,
even the one-legged beauty
topples into insignificance
at the rising thought
of you.

(v) RELATIVE DENSITIES

If I have fallen for you,
it has been
with the improbable weight

of a feather;
the burrowing impudicity
of the flea;
the charm and spin
of a still undiscovered
fundamental particle.

(vi) BIRDSONG

I have been dreaming
in the solitary tree
of your head,
beneath the wet black leaves
of your hair,
of the shining opal
of your breasts.

(vii) "BE FRUITFUL AND MULTIPLY"

I would like to hang
over your lovely dark head,
like a sweetly dipping branch
of your favourite apple tree,
just once.
I would like to pop you,
in your denim jacket,
into a cloning booth,
sending copies
back throughout the ages.

RAIN

Say we went out anyway
under a steady hissing of rain;
say we took the crumbling path
back across the cliffs
above the booming cove;
say we kissed
in the periodic glare
from the lighthouse;
say we climbed the ninety seven steps
to the top of the tower,
undressing as we climbed
and tumbled wet and breathless
onto your welcoming bed;
say you invited me to read
the astonishing astrological predictions
you had had tattooed
on your eloquent skin;
say I am reading still.

ODE 32

(after Catullus)

Give me a call this afternoon
if you have nothing else on,
especially clothes.
We could make love
into the evening and beyond.
Leave the back door off the latch,
tie up that snarling mastiff,
don't change your mind
and go shopping.
Get ready in your room
to come at least nine times
in quick succession,
just for starters.
In fact, I can come over right now.
I'm just lounging on the sofa,
stroking myself,
wondering what to do next
with this twitching erection.

INTO THE SMALL HOURS

Like a drowsy rose
your moistened labials recoil,
petal by glistening petal
after my lingering tonguing.
Your nipples harden around
my throbbing erection
as it thrusts between your cupped,
lightly oiled breasts.
Lowering yourself onto my chest
and locking me into position,
you rub your stiffening clitoris
across my taut, straining pecs.
Then with exquisite deftness
you guide me, inch by swollen inch,
past fold after slippery fold,
into your slurping honeyed core.
And in long shuddering spasms
we come, almost together,
screaming and shouting
the walls of heaven down,
until the milkman's clinking progress
up the empty, starlit street
halts in silent awe
at the front door.

FROM ROMAN ELEGIES
(after Goethe)

Of all the noises that irritate me —
car alarms, Mormons, Cage's 4'33" —
there's nothing as infuriating
as dogs barking late at night.
My sensitive ears are outraged
by their incessant howling.
Though, there is one mangy cur
whose occasional yelp
fills me with delicious anticipation,
since he once barked
at your unexpected arrival.
Now, when I hear him
I think you might be coming
or, better still, I remember a time
I waited for you and you came.

You'll Have to Speak Up

The deaf militia (Beethoven regiment)
are kicking up a racket
beneath my window,
many of them pissed.
I hear that you are still seeing
that handsome young multilinguist,
another thousand kisses missed.

RUSH HOUR

I know the pedestrian light
is in your favour
and you must go and go now
but I want to linger
just a little longer in your embrace
at the corner of Washington Street
and South Main Street.
I want to kiss
each individual hair of your head
from root to tip
while the lights change and change again
and the city grinds to a shuddering halt
and the sky tilts over
to reveal teeming constellations,
utterly silent, unbearably distant.

FURTHER OUT

I can't tell you
where this is happening.
I know it's a dream
because the left bank of the Seine
has just appeared directly opposite
the right bank of the Lee.
I know it's daylight,
or at least dream daylight,
that silver-grey, residual glow
from some imploding star
shining in your glossy black hair.
I know it's you
because there is not one
even remotely as beautiful
on the stony inner planets
and I know you have been kissing me
for over a minute
because I have just woken up
gasping for breath.

LONG VALLEY REVISITED

Middle age is whispering on Winthrop street:
"a taxi, a cup of cocoa and then to bed."
A full moon over Marlboro Street
is exhorting me to stay out,
perk up, think nineteen, get a life!
Trees are stretching into leaf
along the South Mall,
planets are flying wildly past
their preordained perihelia,
bats are fucking frantically in the belfries.
So, I am curling up my toes,
I am sloughing off this ageing skin,
I am kissing Mary Mahony.

WHATEVER HAPPENED TO PATSY COR-BETT?

That was the Summer
the face of the unattainable Marie Flynn
was joined in the crammed pantheon of lust
by the quickly tanning limbs of Patsy Corbett.
When the boys of Mount Farran
tossed off into their socks
through the hot July nights,
dreaming of a first wet kiss
from those lips of a palpable heaven.
That student riotous Summer of '68,
or was it '67?

SEAN GUEVARA LYNCH

When you heard
of Che's execution in Higueras in '67,
did you allow yourself
a little tug of regret,
if only for a long lost kinsman?
Not to mention
a hint of admiration
for his devotion to action,
if not even envy
for his abrupt dispatch.
"There, but for six All Ireland medals
and the millstone of Cork around my neck,
goes Commandante Jack."

A DAY OUT IN SUNDAYS WELL

May 10th, 1851.
A large boisterous crowd in attendance
at the County Gaol
where Catherine Connolly, seventy years of age,
is already poised on the drop
with the rope around her neck.
As she declares her innocence of murder,
the rope is attached to the beam,
the bolt withdrawn
and she is hanged without undue struggling.
Coarse and ribald jests
are bandied about in the crowd.
A popular melody strikes up,
concluding with the refrain:
"She's gone where the good niggers go".

CLEAN EXIT

A good day to die
the laundry basket empty
fresh linen to hand.

ESCAPE

(after Katarzyna Borun)

We set up camp
beside the motorway,
outside the halting-site.
The last hiace van
parked behind bullet-proof glass
in the museum.
Around us, beyond the reach
of calloused hands,
the city howled on its leash.

ABLUTIONS

(after Mandelstam)

I was washing at night in the courtyard,
stars glittered serenely overhead.
Starlight like salt sprinkled on an eyeball,
the rain-butt full and freezing over.

The gates slammed and secured
and the earth truly desolate.
Nothing more pure, more bitter
than truth's empty canvas.

A star melts like sugar in the barrel
and the freezing water seems suddenly deeper.
Death cleaner, misfortune sweeter
and the world more truthful, more terrible.

SLIGHTLY BURNISHED

(i) DARKNESS VISIBLE

In the sky,
a black cloud that steals across
the neon emptiness of the moon.

On my hands,
the useless oils that cannot reach
his rooted legacy of hurt.

In the bathroom,
the gleaming mirrors that reflect
your troubled stare:
futility deepening to despair.

(ii) SLIGHTLY BURNISHED

In the kitchen
an aromatic Boeuf Bourguignon
is simmering over a low flame
as "All Blues" seeps in
from the bedroom
where a bedside lamp
is picking out the henna glints
in your glossy black hair
while you read,
beautiful in glasses,
my hymns to the daughters
of the lower-middle-classes.

THE WOMAN IS ANGRY

(after Gil Vicente)

The woman is angry,
who will speak to her?
The woman walks by the shore,
lonely as the stars,
wrathful as the sea.
The woman is angry,
who will listen to her?

AFTER YEATS

(for Nuala Fenton)

Let them say
what they will.
As far as I'm concerned,
Troy can burn again
for the sake of your exquisite —
oh your exquisite face.
If not Troy,
then at least Thoor Ballylee,
twice.

TORSO OF AN EX-GIRLFRIEND

(after Rainer Maria Rilke)

Too late to know that magnificent head,
eyes like black, fully ripened grapes,
hair, a midnight garden for all the senses.
And yet, the torso seems lit from within,
still holds the gleaming power of her gaze.

With this brilliance, the curves of the breasts
dazzle you, a hint of a smile
shimmers through those thighs to that grove
where all creation falls silent.

This translucence flares out like a dying star,
leaving no shadows, no place where you are
not seen, you must change your life.

PUSHKIN'S ARION

(after Heaney)

We were taking it handy in the boat,
one or two aloft, tweaking the sails,
most of us stretched out on deck,
keeping a watching brief.
Steady and silent she went,
the helmsman humming at his pleasant task.
And I, taking it all for granted,
chanced a popular song.
Then, an incredible blast of air,
a sickening lurch and over we went,
straight to the bottom with all hands.
All except me, thrown clear and washed ashore
on a long cradling swell,
the sea's little joke.
So, here I am on this rocky shore,
gobsmacked at such luck, under a splendid blue sky.
In an hour or so my clothes should be dry.

ON THE ASCENSION OF TSAR NICHOLAS I
(after Pushkin)

Quick to show the intelligentsia
he would take no jive,
he sent one hundred and twenty to Siberia,
strung up five.

PUSHKIN'S MOMENT
(for Síabhra)

July 1st 1832. Peterhof, Empress's birthday.
The Imperial family and court
offer themselves, in their full majesty,
to the public gaze.
As thousands shuffle past
a long line of opulent lineiki,
paying awed homage,
Pushkin, hurrying along
by the side of the road,
is hailed by the Tsar:
"Bonjour Pouchkine,"
"Bonjour Sire," he replies,
without breaking his stride.

FAME
(after Arrian)

Having concluded the formalities
of an alliance with the Celtic tribes
from the Adriatic coast,
Alexander indulges in a little friendly banter:
What, he asks them,
do they fear most in the world,
thinking they must answer,
if only out of politeness,
"You, O Great Lord!"
They reply
that they live in continual terror
of the sky falling on their heads.
Somewhat disappointed and not a little bemused,
Alexander dismisses them,
muttering that they think too much of themselves.
The Celts return home, laughing themselves sick.

NERO'S DEADLINE
(after Cavafy)

When the Delphic Oracle warned Nero:
"Beware the age of seventy three,"
he wasn't unduly concerned.
After all he was only thirty,
plenty of time to prepare
for his future apotheosis.

Now, a trifle weary,
he returns from Achaea.
Deliciously weary,
from a journey devoted exclusively to pleasure:
musical performances, poetry readings, dances,
winning at the Olympic Games no less.
And, of course, plenty of beautiful Greek bodies.

Meanwhile in Spain,
Galba musters and drills a formidable army.
Galba, seventy three yesterday.

THE POET TELLS OF HIS FAME

(after Merwin, after Borges, after el Hadrami)

Limitless space is the measure of my renown,
the libraries of Texas compete for my verse.
Statesmen wait at my hand and my tongue,
angels have already forgotten my work.
The tools of my art are debasement and anguish,
if only I had never been born.

SOME WORDS ON THE DEATH OF WORDSWORTH

On the 23rd of April 1850,
in his eightieth year,
the poet Wordsworth died.
In announcing his demise
"The Democratic Review"
remarked that they
were not impressed
by any heavy sense of sorrow.
They declined to include him
in the list of those who, like Burns,
Byron and Shelley were marked
by their immortal passion for Liberty.
"We have no tears for this salaried
slave of Aristocracy."
"We refuse to mourn the pensioned
parasite of Monarchy."

GOETHE IN HEAVEN

No sooner dead than
hurried by seraphim past
a startled Saint Peter
and swept into the presence of God,
Who, unprompted,
offers Goethe His throne
which Goethe, graciously, accepts.

AFTER SORESCU

A spider's thread
hangs from the ceiling
above my bed.

I watch it inch closer
and closer every day.

It looks as if
they're lowering a ladder
from Heaven for me.

Come on soul, up you go,
I'll be right behind.

AFTER YESENIN

At your funeral
the sky was a tolling bell
its clapper the moon.

AFTER SEFERIS

(for Theo)

As you sleep,
one eye remains open
to the immense choreographies
of the stars,
one ear alert
to the water fretting
at the rudder.

ODYSSEUS RETURNED

And so in Ithaca,
an oar set upright
in a well-tended vineyard
overlooking the wine-dark,
soul-erasing sea.

IN MEMORIAM T.S.ELIOT

The silent rainbird
shakes out his dusty plumage
on the riverbed.

DANTON
(for Paul Durcan)

He surfaced in a gloomy dream,
without his haughty, brutal air.
Slumped by History's bloody stream,
mourning the loss of Robespierre.

THE SIXTH CIRCLE

Farinata,
hailing Dante from his burning tomb,
brings me back :
The soaking pits
in the steel works,
ten feet deep cavities
caked in glistening slag
which we hacked, still hot,
from the steep walls
and shovelled into bins,
until the ladder was lowered
and that infernal foreman
beckoned us
to the surface again.

THE UNINVITED

Forgotten
in the hallway,
the fully laden
coat-stand
is crowded
by ghosts,
each longing
to feel
the lovely weight
of clothes
once again.

SHRED OF MEMORY

A bare arm,
a black dress
glimpsed
behind frosted glass
as I pass
through slanting rain.

HOLY SOULS

November:
here's the ghost of my mother
on her way down to early Mass
followed by the ghost
of her favourite cat
who will wait,
watching for poor ghost mice
from the door of the church,
then follow her
back up the hill
to where the ghost of my father
is preparing breakfast for two
while their real children
sleep fitfully on.

THE POET
(after Alfred de Musset)

It was pitch dark in the "Valley",
I thought I saw a figure
in a white apron
floating above the bar.
It seemed to have come from the keg room,
skimming the tops of those swinging doors
and that famous round table as it came,
but no, it was nothing.

Forget it.

THE POET'S DAY

Aside from the ticking
of the clock
and a late evening breeze
flicking through the pages
of my next book,
there is only the crystalline memory
of you loosening and tying back
your glorious black hair
on the balcony of the restaurant
earlier today;
everything else fades.

DEATH AND RESURRECTION

Beloved Gráinne
in the depths of your cleavage
receive my spirit.

PATIENCE
(after Barthes)

"Wait,"
she promised,
"one hundred nights
beneath my window
and I will be yours."

He waited,
ninety nine nights.

SHIFT

Because he was tired,
he sat down,
his back against the oak tree —
only to wake
to a deep night sky
encrusted with stars;
a sprinkling of rain
cold on his face;
the small glowing hands
on his wrist-watch
spinning backwards.

THE TASK LAID ASIDE

(after Denise Levertov)

or God
as an old man
living upstairs,
watching old movies
at all hours,
letting his apartment fill
with empty beer cans
which he crunches underfoot
as he shuffles about
muttering in Aramaic.

GOD EXPLAINS ETERNAL LIFE

"So I lied...."